ANIMAL ENGINEERS
Bowerbirds

by Rebecca Pettiford

BLASTOFF! READERS 3

BELLWETHER MEDIA • MINNEAPOLIS, MN

Blastoff! Readers are carefully developed by literacy experts to build reading stamina and move students toward fluency by combining standards-based content with developmentally appropriate text.

Level 1 provides the most support through repetition of high-frequency words, light text, predictable sentence patterns, and strong visual support.

Level 2 offers early readers a bit more challenge through varied sentences, increased text load, and text-supportive special features.

Level 3 advances early-fluent readers toward fluency through increased text load, less reliance on photos, advancing concepts, longer sentences, and more complex special features.

★ **Blastoff! Universe**

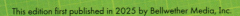

This edition first published in 2025 by Bellwether Media, Inc.

No part of this publication may be reproduced in whole or in part without written permission of the publisher. For information regarding permission, write to Bellwether Media, Inc., Attention: Permissions Department, 6012 Blue Circle Drive, Minnetonka, MN 55343.

Library of Congress Cataloging-in-Publication Data

LC record for Bowerbirds available at: https://lccn.loc.gov/2024015042

Text copyright © 2025 by Bellwether Media, Inc. BLASTOFF! READERS and associated logos are trademarks and/or registered trademarks of Bellwether Media, Inc. Bellwether Media is a division of Chrysalis Education Group.

Editor: Rachael Barnes   Designer: Josh Brink

Printed in the United States of America, North Mankato, MN.

Table of Contents

Bower Builders	4
Planning a Bower	8
Time to Build!	12
The Bower Is Ready!	16
Glossary	22
To Learn More	23
Index	24

Bower Builders

Bowerbirds are songbirds. Males build **bowers** to **attract** females.

Males **decorate** bowers with colorful objects. Then they sing and dance. Successful males **mate** with many females.

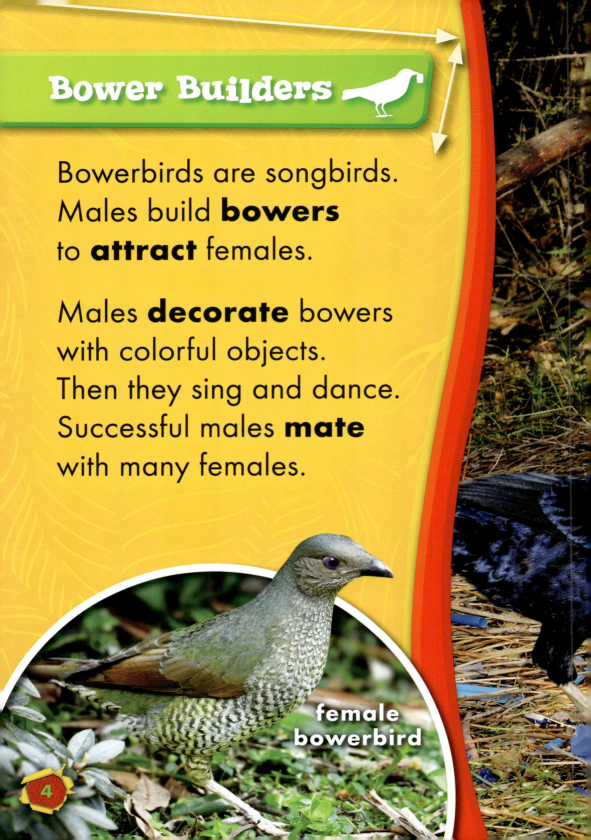

female bowerbird

Bowerbirds live in Australia and New Guinea. They live in **rain forests**, woodlands, and **mangrove swamps**.

satin bowerbird

Satin Bowerbird Range Map

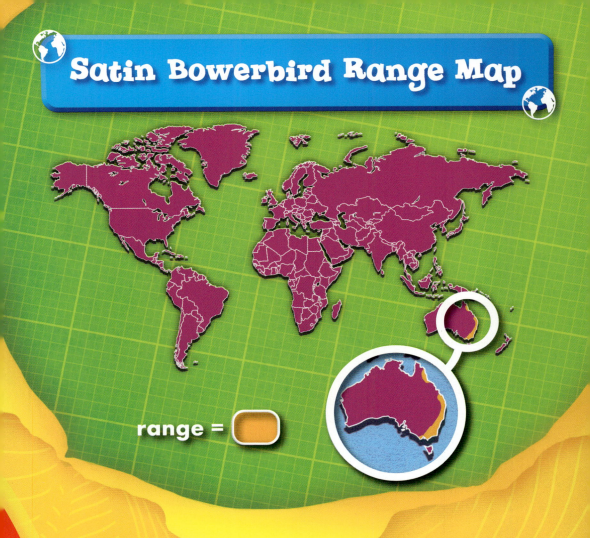

range =

There are about 20 **species** of bowerbirds. Satin bowerbirds are some of the most common.

Planning a Bower

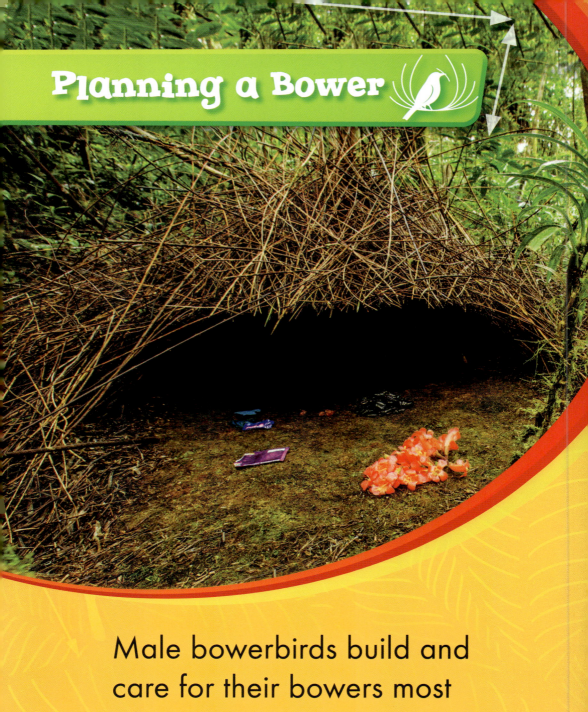

Male bowerbirds build and care for their bowers most of the year. Bowers are built on the ground.

Taller bowers are placed next to trees for support. Satin bowerbirds find shady spots for their bowers.

Some bowerbirds make flat mat bowers. Others **weave** sticks together to build taller bowers.

Maypole bowers are towers of sticks. Some have huge roofs. Avenue bowers have two separate walls. There is an opening in the middle.

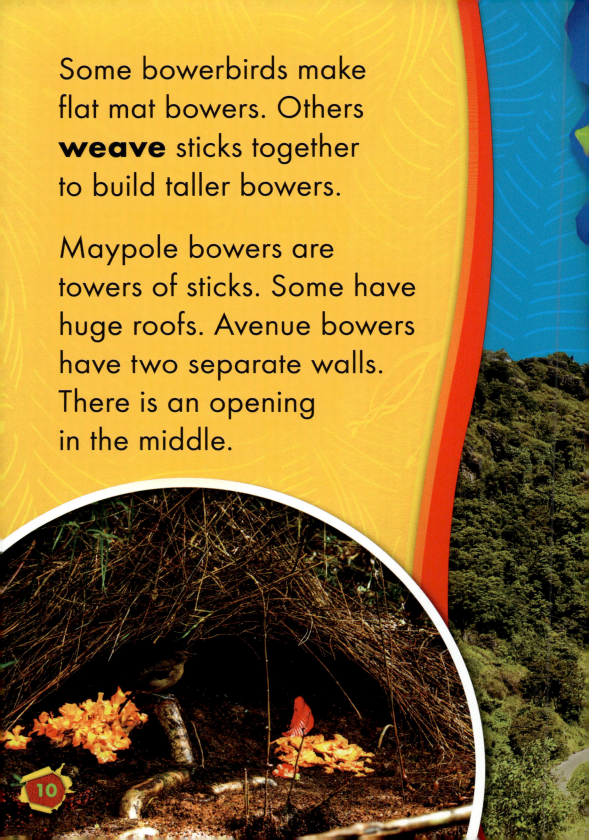

Types of Bowers

- avenue and mat bowers look alike across different bowerbird species

- maypole bowers can look very different, but they all have a support in the center

avenue bower

mat bower

maypole bowers

Time to Build!

Males that build maypole or avenue bowers gather sticks. They use their beaks to push some sticks into the ground.

Building Tools

beak

saliva

They weave other sticks to make walls. Sometimes males paint the walls with a mix of plants and **saliva**.

It is time to decorate! Popular objects are flowers, berries, and feathers. Males will also use glass and plastic!

decorations

Decorating Materials

flowers

berries

feathers

plastic

They gather many objects and return to the bower. They put objects in and around the bower.

The Bower Is Ready!

Males carefully place their objects in **patterns** that females might enjoy. They will often move objects again and again.

It can take one to eight weeks to get the bower ready.

When a female arrives, the male dances and **struts**. He chatters and makes other loud sounds. He offers her objects from his collection.

If she is pleased,
she enters the bower.

After the birds mate, the female leaves. She builds a nest for her eggs. The male stays and prepares his bower for another female.

Some male bowerbirds care for the same bower for over 30 years!

Glossary

attract—to draw attention and interest

bowers—structures that male bowerbirds build to attract female bowerbirds

decorate—to add something to an object or place to make it beautiful

mangrove swamps—coastal saltwater wetlands filled with tropical trees called mangroves

mate—to join together to make young

patterns—sets of forms or shapes that repeat

rain forests—thick, green forests that receive a lot of rain

saliva—a watery liquid made in the mouth

species—kinds of animals

struts—walks in a proud way

weave—to form by passing strips of materials over and under each other

To Learn More

AT THE LIBRARY

Cherrix, Amy. *Animal Architects*. New York, N.Y.: Beach Lane Books, 2021.

Pettiford, Rebecca. *Weavers*. Minneapolis, Minn.: Bellwether Media, 2025.

Roth, Susan L. *Birds of a Feather: Bowerbirds and Me*. New York, N.Y.: Neal Porter Books/Holiday House, 2019.

ON THE WEB

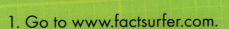

Factsurfer.com gives you a safe, fun way to find more information.

1. Go to www.factsurfer.com.

2. Enter "bowerbirds" into the search box and click 🔍.

3. Select your book cover to see a list of related content.

Index

Australia, 6
beaks, 12
bowers, 4, 5, 8, 9, 10, 11, 12, 15, 17, 19, 20, 21
building tools, 13
dance, 4, 18
decorate, 4, 14
decorating materials, 15
eggs, 20
females, 4, 16, 18, 20
ground, 8, 12
males, 4, 8, 12, 13, 14, 16, 18, 20, 21
mangrove swamps, 6
mate, 4, 20
nest, 20
New Guinea, 6
objects, 4, 14, 15, 16, 18
paint, 13
patterns, 16
plants, 13

rain forests, 6
range, 6, 7
roofs, 10
saliva, 13
satin bowerbirds, 7, 9
sing, 4
songbirds, 4
sounds, 18
species, 7
sticks, 10, 12, 13
struts, 18
types of bowers, 11
walls, 10, 13
weave, 10, 13
woodlands, 6

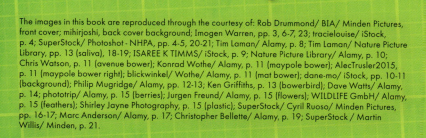

The images in this book are reproduced through the courtesy of: Rob Drummond/ BIA/ Minden Pictures, front cover; mihirjoshi, back cover background; Imogen Warren, pp. 3, 6-7, 23; tracielouise/ iStock, p. 4; SuperStock/ Photoshot - NHPA, pp. 4-5, 20-21; Tim Laman/ Alamy, p. 8; Tim Laman/ Nature Picture Library, pp. 13 (saliva), 18-19; ISAREE K TIMMS/ iStock, p. 9; Nature Picture Library/ Alamy, p. 10; Chris Watson, p. 11 (avenue bower); Konrad Wothe/ Alamy, p. 11 (maypole bower); AlecTrusler2015, p. 11 (maypole bower right); blickwinkel/ Wothe/ Alamy, p. 11 (mat bower); dane-mo/ iStock, pp. 10-11 (background); Philip Mugridge/ Alamy, pp. 12-13; Ken Griffiths, p. 13 (bowerbird); Dave Watts/ Alamy, p. 14; phototrip/ Alamy, p. 15 (berries); Jurgen Freund/ Alamy, p. 15 (flowers); WILDLIFE GmbH/ Alamy, p. 15 (feathers); Shirley Jayne Photography, p. 15 (plastic); SuperStock/ Cyril Ruoso/ Minden Pictures, pp. 16-17; Marc Anderson/ Alamy, p. 17; Christopher Bellette/ Alamy, p. 19; SuperStock / Martin Willis/ Minden, p. 21.